Beastly Boys and Ghastly Girls

Poems Collected by William Cole

Drawings by Tomi Ungerer

Beastly Boys
and Ghastly Girls

MAMMOTH

First published in Great Britain 1970
by Methuen & Co Ltd
Paperback edition first published 1975 by
Methuen Children's Books Ltd
Reprinted as a Magnet paperback 1979
Reprinted 1980
Published 1990 by Mammoth
an imprint of Mandarin Paperbacks
Michelin House, 81 Fulham Road, London SW3 6RB
Reprinted 1990 (twice)

Mandarin is an imprint of the Octopus Publishing Group

ISBN 0 7497 0275 3

A CIP catalogue record for this title
is available from the British Library

Printed in Great Britain
by Cox & Wyman Ltd, Reading, Berkshire

Macmillan & Co Ltd, for "Little Thomas" and "Matilda" from *Puffin, Puma & Co* by F. Gwynne Evans. Reprinted by permission of Macmillan & Co Ltd.

Methuen & Co Ltd, for "Rice Pudding" from *When We Were Very Young* by A. A. Milne, copyright 1924 by A. A. Milne, and "The Good Little Girl" from *Now We Are Six* by A. A. Milne, copyright 1927 by A. A. Milne. Reprinted by permission of Methuen & Co Ltd and the A. A. Milne estate. Also for "Dirge for a Bad Boy" and "Two People" from *The Flattered Flying Fish* by E. C. Rieu, copyright © 1962 by E. V. Rieu. Reprinted by permission of Methuen & Co Ltd.

The New Yorker Magazine Inc, for "Psychological Prediction" by Virginia Brasier, copyright © 1942 The New Yorker Magazine Inc, Reprinted by permission of the New Yorker Magazine Inc and the author.

Oxford University Press, for "Piano Practice" from *Happily Ever After* by Ian Serraillier. Reprinted by permission of Oxford University Press.

A. D. Peters, for "Henry King" and "Jim" from *Cautionary Verses* by Hilaire Belloc. Reprinted by permission of A. D. Peters.

Rand McNally & Company, publishers, for "Jelly Jake and Butter Bill" and "Polly Picklenose" from the *Peter Patter Book* by Leroy F. Jackson, copyright 1918, renewal 1946 by Rand McNally & Company, publishers. Reprinted by permission of Rand McNally & Company.

Routledge & Kegan Paul Ltd, for "Jane, Do Be Careful" by Irene Page from *Poems by Children* by Michael Baldwin. Reprinted by permission of Routledge & Kegan Paul Ltd.

Shelley Silverstein, for his poems "Sarah Cynthia Sylvia Stout," "Think of Eight Numbers From One to Nine," and "Nothing To Do?" Reprinted by permission of the author.

The Society of Authors as the literary representative of the Estate of A. E. Housman, and Jonathan Cape Ltd, publishers of *A. E. Housman* by Laurence Housman, for "Inhuman Henry", copyright 1938 by Laurence Housman. Reprinted by permission of The Society of Authors and Jonathan Cape Ltd.

The World Publishing Company, for "Baby Toodles" from *Verse Yet!* by Joseph S. Newman, copyright © 1959 by Joseph S. Newman. Reprinted by permission of The World Publishing Company.

Contents

AND BEAT HIM WHEN HE SNEEZES

Here in this book, collected for you,
Are hundreds of things that you never should do,
Like stewing your sister, scaring your brother,
Or disobeying your father or mother.

I've heard there are children who never are bad;
Who never act sullen or snippy or sad;
Who always say "Thank you," and sit up real straight,
And never are lazy and never are late;
Who never would dream to be sassy or bold,
And go to bed early, and do as they're told;
Who won't touch a thing if they're told "Don't you touch!"
    Do I like that kind of children?

                                        Not much!

For it isn't normal to always be good—
I don't think you'd want to, and don't think you should;
Just as food tastes better with a shake of salt,
A small bit of mischief is hardly a fault.
And life would be boring, and life would be grim,
If children were all goody-goody and prim.
For children will tickle, and poke, and wiggle,
And just when they're not supposed to, they'll giggle;
And they are inclined to make much too much noise
(This is true of the girls—but, goodness! The boys!)

*   *   *

Most of these poems and illustrations
Are very much ex-ag-ger-a-tions;
Meaning that no one would ever do
Such wicked and horrid things. . . . would you?
Of course you wouldn't . . . but listen . . . look . . .
If ever you do—*Don't Blame This Book!*

WILLIAM COLE

Put Some Mustard
in Your Shoe

Bringing Him Up

(to be read solemnly)

Mister Thomas Jones
Said to James, his son:
"Never swallow bones,
Never point a gun.

Never slam a door,
Never play with flames,
Never shun the poor."
"*Dull* old fool!" said James.

LORD DUNSANY

Nothing To Do?

Nothing to do?
Nothing to do?
Put some mustard in your shoe,
Fill your pockets full of soot,
Drive a nail into your foot,
Put some sugar in your hair,
Place your toys upon the stair,
Smear some jelly on the latch,
Eat some mud and strike a match,
Draw a picture on the wall,

Roll some marbles down the hall,
Pour some ink in daddy's cap—
Now go upstairs and take a nap.

SHELLEY SILVERSTEIN

The Boy Who Laughed at Santa Claus

In Baltimore there lived a boy.
He wasn't anybody's joy.
Although his name was Jabez Dawes,
His character was full of flaws.
In school he never led his classes,
He hid old ladies' reading glasses,
His mouth was open when he chewed,
And elbows to the table glued.

He stole the milk of hungry kittens,
And walked through doors marked NO ADMITTANCE.

He said he acted thus because
There wasn't any Santa Claus.
Another trick that tickled Jabez
Was crying "Boo!" at little babies.
He brushed his teeth, they said in town,
Sideways instead of up and down.

Yet people pardoned every sin,
And viewed his antics with a grin,
Till they were told by Jabez Dawes,
"There isn't any Santa Claus!"
Deploring how he did behave,
His parents swiftly sought their grave.
They hurried through the portals pearly,
And Jabez left the funeral early.

Like whooping cough, from child to child,
He sped to spread the rumor wild:
"Sure as my name is Jabez Dawes
There isn't any Santa Claus!"
Slunk like a weasel or a marten
Through nursery and kindergarten,
Whispering low to every tot,
"There isn't any, no there's not!"

The children wept all Christmas Eve
And Jabez chortled up his sleeve.
No infant dared hang up his stocking
For fear of Jabez' ribald mocking.
He sprawled on his untidy bed,
Fresh malice dancing in his head,
When presently with scalp a-tingling,
Jabez heard a distant jingling;
He heard the crunch of sleigh and hoof
Crisply alighting on the roof.

What good to rise and bar the door?
A shower of soot was on the floor.
What was beheld by Jabez Dawes?
The fireplace full of Santa Claus!
Then Jabez fell upon his knees
With cries of "Don't," and "Pretty please."
He howled, "I don't know where you read it,
But anyhow, I never said it!"

"Jabez," replied the angry saint,
"It isn't I, it's you that ain't.

Although there is a Santa Claus,
There isn't any Jabez Dawes!"
Said Jabez then with impudent vim,
"Oh, yes there is; and I am him!
Your magic don't scare me, it doesn't"—
And suddenly he found he wasn't!

From grimy feet to grimy locks,
Jabez became a Jack-in-the-box,
An ugly toy with springs unsprung,
Forever sticking out his tongue.
The neighbours heard his mournful squeal;
They searched for him, but not with zeal.
No trace was found of Jabez Dawes,
Which led to thunderous applause,
And people drank a loving cup
And went and hung their stockings up.

All you who sneer at Santa Claus,
Beware the fate of Jabez Dawes,
The saucy boy who mocked the saint.
Donder and Blitzen licked off his paint.

OGDEN NASH

Oh, No!

Oh, no!
'Tisn't so!
Papa's watch
Won't go?

It *must* go—
Guess I know!
Last night
I wound it tight,
And greased it nice
With camphor-ice.

MARY MAPES DODGE

The Opportune Overthrow of Humpty Dumpty

Upon a wall of medium height
   Bombastically sat
A boastful boy, and he was quite
   Unreasonably fat:
And what aroused a most intense
   Disgust in passers-by
Was his abnormal impudence
   In hailing them with "Hi!"
While by his kicks he loosened bricks
   The girls to terrify.

When thus for half an hour or more
   He'd played his idle tricks,
And wounded something like a score

Of people with the bricks,
A man who kept a fuel shop
   Across from where he sat
Remarked: "Well, this has got to stop."
   Then, snatching up his hat,
And sallying out, began to shout:
   "Look here! Come down from that!"

The boastful boy to laugh began,
   As laughs a vapid clown,
And cried: "It takes a bigger man
   Than you to call me down!
This wall is smooth, this wall is high,
   And safe from every one.
No acrobat could do what I
   Had been and gone and done!"
Though this reviled, the other smiled,
   And said: "Just wait, my son!"

Then, to the interested throng
   That watched across the way
He showed with smiling face a long
   And slender Henry Clay,
Remarking: "In upon my shelves
   All kinds of coal there are.
Step in, my friends, and help yourselves.
   And he who first can jar
That wretched urchin off his perch
   Will get this good cigar."

The throng this task did not disdain,
    But threw with heart and soul,
Till round the youth there raged a rain
    Of lumps of cannel-coal.
He dodged for all that he was worth,
    Till one bombarder deft
Triumphant brought him down to earth,
    Of vanity bereft.
"I see," said he, "that this is the
    Coal day when I get left."

The moral is that fuel can
    Become the tool of fate
When thrown upon a little man,
    Instead of on a grate.
This story proves that when a brat
    Imagines he's admired,
And acts in such a fashion that
    He makes his neighbours tired,
That little fool, who's much too cool,
    Gets warmed when coal is fired.

GUY WETMORE CARRYL

Psychological Prediction

I think little Louie will turn out a crook. He
Puts on rubber gloves when stealing a cookie.

VIRGINIA BRASIER

Two People

Two people live in Rosamund,
   And one is very nice;
The other is devoted
   To every kind of vice—

To walking where the puddles are,
   And eating far too quick,
And saying words she shouldn't know,
   And wanting spoons to lick.

Two people live in Rosamund,
   And one (I say it twice)
Is very nice *and* very good:
   The other's only nice.

E. V. RIEU

Johnny Went to Church One Day

Johnny went to church one day,
   He climbed up in the steeple;
He took his shoes and stockings off
   And threw them at the people.

FOLK RHYME

Inhuman Henry
or
Cruelty to Fabulous Animals

Oh would you know why Henry sleeps,
And why his mourning Mother weeps,
And why his weeping Mother mourns?
He was unkind to unicorns.

No unicorn, with Henry's leave,
Could dance upon the lawn at eve,
Or gore the gardener's boy in spring
Or do the very slightest thing.

No unicorn could safely roar,
And dash its nose against the door,
Nor sit in peace upon the mat
To eat the dog, or drink the cat.

Henry would never in the least
Encourage the heraldic beast:
If there were unicorns about
He went and let the lion out.

The lion, leaping from its chain
And glaring through its tangled mane,
Would stand on end and bark and bound
And bite what unicorns it found.

And when the lion bit a lot
Was Henry sorry? He was not.
What did his jumps betoken? Joy.
He was a bloody-minded boy.

The Unicorn is not a Goose,
And when they saw the lion loose
They grew increasingly aware
That they had better not be there.

And oh, the unicorn is fleet
And spurns the earth with all its feet.
The lion had to snap and snatch
At tips of tails it could not catch.

Returning home in temper bad,
It met the sanguinary lad,
And clasping Henry with its claws
It took his legs between its jaws.

"Down, lion, down!" said Henry, "cease!
My legs immediately release."
His formidable feline pet
Made no reply, but only ate.

The last words that were ever said
By Henry's disappearing head,
In accents of indignant scorn,
Were "I am not a unicorn."

And now you know why Henry sleeps,
And why his Mother mourns and weeps,
And why she also weeps and mourns;
So now be kind to unicorns.

A. E. HOUSMAN

My Brother Bert

Pets are the Hobby of my brother Bert.
He used to go to school with a Mouse in his shirt.

His Hobby it grew, as some hobbies will,
And grew and GREW and GREW until—

Oh don't breathe a word, pretend you haven't heard.
A simply appalling thing has occurred—

The very thought makes me iller and iller:
Bert's brought home a gigantic Gorilla!

If you think that's really not such a scare,
What if it quarrels with his Grizzly Bear?

You still think you could keep your head?
What if the Lion from under the bed

And the four Ostriches that deposit
Their football eggs in his bedroom closet

And the Aardvark out of his bottom drawer
All danced out and joined in the Roar?

What if the Pangolins were to caper
Out of their nests behind the wallpaper?

With the fifty sorts of Bats
That hang on his hatstand like old hats,

And out of a shoebox the excitable Platypus
Along with the Ocelot or Jungle-Cattypus?

The Wombat, the Dingo, the Gecko, the Grampus—
How they would shake the house with their Rumpus!

Not to forget the Bandicoot
Who would certainly peer from his battered old boot.

Why it could be a dreadful day,
And what Oh what would the neighbours say!

TED HUGHES

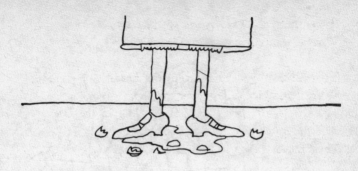

Two Limericks

There was a young girl of Asturias,
Whose temper was frantic and furious.
    She used to throw eggs
    At her grandmother's legs—
A habit unpleasant, but curious.

There was a young lady of Oakham,
Who would steal your cigars and then soak 'em
    In honey and rum,
    And then smear 'em with gum,
So it wasn't a pleasure to smoke 'em.

ANONYMOUS

Think of Eight Numbers

Think of eight numbers from one to nine—
That's fine.
Now pick up the phone and dial them all—
That's making a call.
Now wait till somebody answers,
Then shout "Yickety-yick!" and hang up quick,
And sit for awhile,
And have a smile,
And start all over again.

SHELLEY SILVERSTEIN

Wriggling, Giggling, Noise, and Tattling

Polly, Dolly, Kate and Molly

Polly, Dolly, Kate and Molly,
All are filled with pride and folly.
    Polly tattles,
    Dolly wriggles,
    Katy rattles,
    Molly giggles;
Whoever knew such constant rattling,
Wriggling, giggling, noise, and tattling.

ANONYMOUS

Jittery Jim

There's room on the bus
For the two of us,
But not for Jittery Jim.

He has a train
And a rocket plane,
He has a seal
That can bark and swim,

And a centipede
With wiggly legs,
And an ostrich
Sitting on ostrich eggs,
And crawfish
Floating in oily kegs!

There's room in the bus
For the two of us,
But we'll shut the door on *him!*

WILLIAM JAY SMITH

Dan Dunder

Dan Dunder is a blunder.
What makes Dan so loud, I wonder?
If *I* knew how to be that loud
I think I'd look for a big black cloud
And get a job with it—as thunder!

JOHN CIARDI

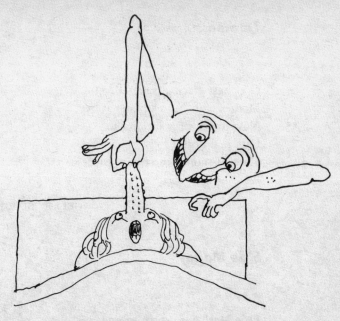

Polly Picklenose

"Polly, Polly, goodness gracious!
You just quit your making faces."
Polly laughed at what they said,
Cocked her nose and went to bed.

But the big black Bugoo heard,
And he came without a word;
Walked right in—you bet a nickel!
In his hand a great green pickle;

Stalked along with steady pace,
Stuck it right in Polly's face,
Pinned it fast, and there it grows—
Poor Polly Picklenose!

LEROY F. JACKSON

Tardiness

Goodness gracious sakes alive!
Mother said, "Come home at five!"
Now the clock is striking six,
I am in a norful fix!
She will think I can't be trusted,
And she'll say that she's disgusted!

GELETT BURGESS

Elsie Marley

Elsie Marley is grown so fine,
She won't get up to feed the swine.
But lies in bed till eight or nine.
    Lazy Elsie Marley.

ENGLISH NURSERY RHYME

The Sad Story of a Little Boy That Cried

Once a little boy, Jack, was, oh! ever so good,
Till he took a strange notion to cry all he could.

So he cried all the day, and he cried all the night,
He cried in the morning and in the twilight;

He cried till his voice was as hoarse as a crow,
And his mouth grew so large it looked like a great O.

It grew at the bottom, and grew at the top;
It grew till they thought that it never would stop.

Each day his great mouth grew taller and taller,
And his dear little self grew smaller and smaller.

At last, that same mouth grew so big that—alack!—
It was only a mouth with a border of Jack.

ANONYMOUS

The Good Little Girl

It's funny how often they say to me, "Jane?
  "Have you been a *good* girl?"
  "Have you been a *good* girl?"
And when they have said it, they say it again,
  "Have you been a *good* girl?"
  "Have you been a *good* girl?"

I go to a party, I go out to tea,
I go to an aunt for a week at the sea,
I come back from school or from playing a game;

Wherever I come from, it's always the same:
  "Well?
  Have you been a *good* girl, Jane?"

It's always the end of the loveliest day:
  "Have you been a *good* girl?"
  "Have you been a *good* girl?"
I went to the Zoo, and they waited to say:
  "Have you been a *good* girl?"
  "Have you been a *good* girl?"

Well, what do they think that I went there to do?
And why should I want to be bad at the Zoo?
And should I be likely to say if I had?
So that's why it's funny of Mummy and Dad,
This asking and asking, in case I was bad.
  "Well?
  Have you been a *good* girl, Jane?"

A. A. MILNE

Lazy Lou

Lazy Lou, Lazy Lou,
What's the matter, child, with you?
Can't you work? Can't you play?
Can't you tuck your hair away?
If I were you, my Lazy Lou,
I'd change my ways. That's what I'd do.

MARY MAPES DODGE

Felicia Ropps

Funny, how Felicia Ropps
Always handles things in shops!
Always pinching, always poking,
Always feeling, always stroking
Things she has no right to touch!
Goops like that annoy me much!

GELETT BURGESS

Children When They're Very Sweet

Children, when they're very sweet,
    Only bite and scratch and kick
A very little. Just enough
    To show their parents they're not sick.

After all if children should
    (By some horrible mistake)
Be entirely good all day
    Every parent's heart would ache.

"Our little monsters must be ill:
    They're much too well behaved!
Call the doctor! Do it quick!
    Maybe they can still be saved!

. . . Wait! They're looking better now.
    Johnny just kicked Billy's shin!
Betty just bit Teddy's ear!
    Jane just stuck me with a pin!

There! The little dears are fit
    As sharks and crocodiles, you'll find.
No need for the doctor now:
    Get a stick and make them mind!"

JOHN CIARDI

They Spill Their Broth
on the Tablecloth

Table Manners

The Goops they lick their fingers,
    And the Goops they lick their knives;
They spill their broth on the table-cloth;
    Oh, they live untidy lives.
The Goops they talk while eating,
    And loud and fast they chew,
So that is why I am glad that I
    Am not a Goop. Are you?

GELETT BURGESS

Little Thomas

Thomas was a little glutton
Who took four times beef or mutton,
Then undid a lower button
      And consumed plum-duff,
And when he could scarcely swallow
Asked if there was more to follow,
As he'd still a tiny hollow
      That he'd like to stuff.

He was told: "You won't get thinner
While you will eat so much dinner;
If you don't take care, some inner
      Part of you will burst."
He replied: "What does it matter
Even if I do get fatter?
Put more pudding on my platter:
      Let it do its worst."

Then one day, and little wonder,
There was a report like thunder:
Doors and windows flew asunder,
      And the cat had fits.
As his anxious friends foreboded,
Dangerously overloaded
Thomas had at length exploded,
      And was blown to bits.

His old nurse cried, much disgusted,
"There, just when I've swept and dusted,
Drat the boy! he's gone and busted,
      Making such a mess";
While the painful task of peeling
Thomas off the walls and ceiling
Gave his family a feeling
      Of sincere distress.

When a boy, who so obese is,
Scatters into tiny pieces,
And the cause of his decease is
      Having overdined,
It is hard to send a version
Of the facts of his dispersion
To the papers for insertion
      Which will be refined.

Any sorrowing relation
Asked for an elucidation
Of the awful detonation
      Was obliged to say:
"Germans have not been to bomb us:
It was only little Thomas,
Who, alas! departed from us
      In that noisy way."

F. GWYNNE EVANS

Henry King,

WHO CHEWED BITS OF STRING,
AND WAS EARLY CUT OFF IN DREADFUL AGONIES

The Chief Defect of Henry King
Was chewing little bits of String.
At last he swallowed some which tied
Itself in ugly Knots inside.
Physicians of the Utmost Fame
Were called at once; but when they came
They answered, as they took their Fees,
"There is no Cure for this Disease.
Henry will very soon be dead."
His Parents stood about his Bed
Lamenting his Untimely Death,
When Henry, with his Latest Breath,
Cried—"Oh, my Friends, be warned by me,
That Breakfast, Dinner, Lunch and Tea
Are all the Human Frame requires . . ."
With that the Wretched Child expires.

HILAIRE BELLOC

The Story of Augustus,

WHO WOULD NOT HAVE ANY SOUP

Augustus was a chubby lad;
Fat, ruddy cheeks Augustus had;
And everybody saw with joy
The plump and hearty, healthy boy.
He ate and drank as he was told,
And never let his soup get cold.

But one day—one cold winter's day,
He screamed out—"Take the soup away!
Oh take the nasty soup away!
I *won't* have any soup to-day."

Next day begins his tale of woes;
Quite lank and lean Augustus grows.
Yet, though he feels so weak and ill,
The naughty fellow cries out still—
"Not any soup for me, I say:
Oh take the nasty soup away!
I *won't* have any soup to-day."

The third day comes: Oh what a sin!
To make himself so pale and thin.
Yet, when the soup is put on table,
He screams, as loud as he is able,
"Not any soup for me, I say:
Oh take the nasty soup away!
I-won't-have-any-soup-to-day."

Look at him, now the fourth day's come!
He scarcely weighs a sugar-plum;
He's like a little bit of thread,
And on the fifth day, he was—dead!

HEINRICH HOFFMANN

Baby Toodles

Alphabet noodles
For Baby Toodles . . .
Alphabet noodles!

HEY!
What's Toodles about?
Why, she's spitting them out!

Mama said,
(As she walloped her over the head)
"Toodles! . . .
Those *wonderful* alphabet noodles!
I'll send you to bed . . .
That's what I'll do,
At the very next *word* out of you!"

JOSEPH S. NEWMAN

The Visitor

John's manners at the table
    Were very sad to see.
You'd scarce believe a child could act
    In such a way as he.

He smacked his lips and gobbled,
    His nose down in his plate.
You might have thought that he was starved,
    So greedily he ate.

He'd snatch for what he wanted,
    And never once say "please,"

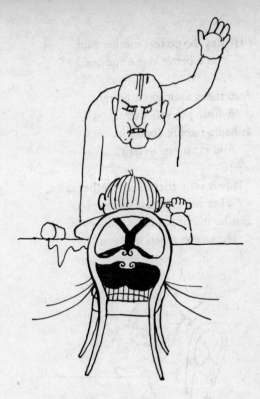

Or, elbows on the table,
    He'd sit and take his ease.

In vain papa reproved him;
    In vain mamma would say,
"You really ought to be ashamed
    To eat in such a way."

One day when lunch was ready,
    And John came in from play,
His mother said, "A friend has come
    To eat with you today."

"A friend of mine?" cried Johnny,
    "Whoever can it be?"

"He's at the table," mother said,
  "You'd better come and see."

Into the dining room he ran.
  A little pig was there.
It had a napkin round its neck,
  And sat up in a chair.

"This is your friend," his father cried,
  "He's just a pig, it's true,
But he might really be your twin,
  He acts so much like you."

"Indeed he's *not* my friend," cried John,
  With red and angry face.
"If he sits there beside my chair
  I'm going to change my place."

"No, no," his father quickly cried,
  "Indeed that will not do.
Sit down at once where you belong,
  He's come to visit *you*."

Now how ashamed was little John;
  But there he had to sit,
And see the piggy served with food,
  And watch him gobble it.

"John," said mamma, "I think your friend
  Would like a piece of bread."
"And pass him the potatoes, too,"
  Papa politely said.

The other children laughed at this,
  But father shook his head.
"Be still, or leave the room at once;
  It's not a joke," he said.

"Oh mother, send the pig away,"
  With tears cried little John.
"I'll never eat that way again.
  If only he'll be gone."

"Why," said mamma, "since that's the case
  And you your ways will mend,
Perhaps we'd better let him go.
  Perhaps he's not your friend."

Now John has learned his lesson,
  For ever since that day
He's lost his piggish manners,
  And eats the proper way.

And his papa, and his mother too,
  Are both rejoiced to see
How mannerly and how polite
  Their little John can be.

KATHERINE PYLE

Jane, Do Be Careful

"Oh, Jane, do be careful!
  You've spilt the milk
  You've drowned the cat,
Jane, do be careful.

"Oh, Jane, do be careful!
  Look at that ink
  In the dog's drink.
Jane, do be careful.

"Oh, Jane, do be careful!
  You spend money galore
  It makes your dad sore,
Jane, do be careful.

"Oh, Jane, do be careful!
  You'll sorrow for this
  You'll sorrow for that,
Jane, do be careful."

IRENE PAGE
(Age 10)

Slovenly Peter

Shock-headed Peter! There he stands,
With his horrid hair and hands.
See, his nails are never cut;
They are grimed as black as soot;
And, the sloven, I declare,
He has never combed his hair;
Anything to me is sweeter
Than to see Shock-headed Peter.

HEINRICH HOFFMANN

Jelly Jake and Butter Bill

Jelly Jake and Butter Bill
One dark night when all was still
Pattered down the long, dark stair,
And no one saw the guilty pair;

Pushed aside the pantry-door
And there found everything galore,—
Honey, raisins, orange-peel,
Cold chicken aplenty for a meal,
Gingerbread enough to fill
Two such boys as Jake and Bill.
Well, they ate and ate and ate,
Gobbled at an awful rate
Till I'm sure they soon weighed more
Than double what they did before.
And then, it's awful, still it's true,
The floor gave way and they went through.
Filled so full they couldn't fight,
Slowly they sank out of sight.
Father, Mother, Cousin Ann,
Cook and nurse and furnace man

Fished in forty-dozen ways
After them, for twenty days;
But not a soul has chanced to get
A glimpse or glimmer of them yet.
And I'm afraid we never will—
Poor Jelly Jake and Butter Bill.

LEROY F. JACKSON

The Sweet Tooth

A sweet tooth was our Frederick.
　He scorned the bread and meat
And all the other wholesome things
　That children ought to eat.

He ate the sugar from the bowl;
　He fed on cakes and pies,
The very sight of lollipops
　Brought water to his eyes.

He grew too fat to play about,
　Too fat to run or jump,
On either side his arms stuck out
　Like handles of a pump.

It grieved his kind mama to see
  How fat and fatter grew
Her little Fred, in spite of all
  That she could say or do.

One day, with pennies in his hand
  He set out for a shop,
To buy himself some sugarcakes
  Or tart or lollipop.

But oh the day was very hot,
  The sun a fiery ball,
And soon the heat made Fred so soft
  He scarce could walk at all.

"Oh dear, oh dear! I feel so queer;
  What's happening?" cried he.
"If I should melt in all this heat
  How dreadful it would be!"

It is a sorry tale to tell,
  But greedy ones take heed!
Fred's arms and legs and all of him
  Were melting down indeed.

They melted till you scarce could tell
  Fred was a boy at all,
For now he looked all smooth and round
  As though he were a ball.

That afternoon the girls and boys
  Came running out to play,
And wondering they gathered round
  The place where Frederick lay.

"Oh what a great enormous ball!
  "Let's play with it," they cried;

And then they rolled and pushed poor Fred
  About from side to side.

Hither and yon, in giddy round
  The wretched Frederick sped,
And sometimes he was on his heels,
  And sometimes on his head.

At supper time the mothers called,
"Now put your ball away.
Tomorrow you can get it out
And have another play."

Ah Frederick, poor Frederick!
Though he lay quiet now
He could not even lift his hand
To wipe his heated brow.

And now each day they came to play
With Fred, until at last
His fat began to wear away
They rolled him round so fast.

The disappointed children said,
"Someone has spoiled our ball.
It's growing such a funny shape
It scarcely rolls at all."

One time when they had stopped to rest
Fred's little brother said,
"It's queer, but don't you think our ball
Looks very much like Fred?"

"Why it is Fred," his sister cried.
"I know his eyes and nose.
And only see! Those are his hands,
And down there are his toes."

They called his mother out to see.
   With eager steps she came,
At once she knew her Frederick,
   And called him by his name.

And now he found that he could turn,
   That he could move and rise.
He stood before his mother
   With shamed and tearful eyes.

"Oh, mother, mother, dear, I've had
   A dreadful time!" cried he,
"But now that I'm a boy again
   Less greedy I will be."

KATHERINE PYLE

Rice Pudding

What is the matter with Mary Jane?
She's crying with all her might and main,
And she won't eat her dinner—rice pudding again—
What *is* the matter with Mary Jane?

What is the matter with Mary Jane?
I've promised her dolls and a daisy-chain,
And a book about animals—all in vain—
What *is* the matter with Mary Jane?

What is the matter with Mary Jane?
She's perfectly well, and she hasn't a pain;
But, look at her, now she's beginning again!—
What *is* the matter with Mary Jane?

What is the matter with Mary Jane?
I've promised her sweets and a ride in the train,
And I've begged her to stop for a bit and explain—
What *is* the matter with Mary Jane?

What is the matter with Mary Jane?
She's perfectly well and she hasn't a pain,
And it's lovely rice pudding for dinner again!—
What *is* the matter with Mary Jane?

A. A. MILNE

The Naughtiest Children I Know

Extremely Naughty Children

By far
The naughtiest
Children
I know
Are Jasper
Geranium
James
And Jo.

They live
In a house
On the Hill
Of Kidd,
And what
In the world
Do you think
They did?

They asked
Their Uncles
And Aunts
To tea,
And shouted
In loud,
Rude voices
"We

Are tired
Of scoldings
And sendings
To bed;
Now
The grown-ups
Shall be
Punished instead."

They said:
"Auntie Em,
You didn't
Say 'Thank you!' "
They said:
"Uncle Robert,
We're going
To spank you!"

They pulled
The beard
Of Sir Henry
Dorner
And put him
To stand
In disgrace
In the corner.

They scolded
Aunt B.
They punished
Aunt Jane;
They slapped
Aunt Louisa
Again
And again.

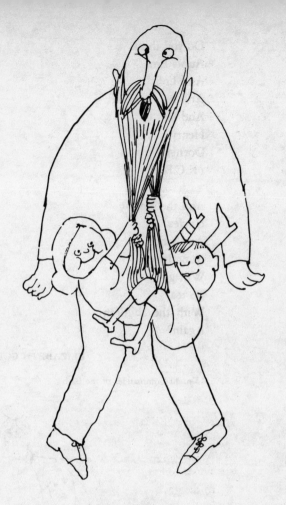

They said
"Naughty boy!"
To their
Uncle
Fred,
And boxed
His ears
And sent him
To bed.

Do you think
Aunts Em
And Loo
And B.,
And Sir
Henry
Dorner
(K.C.B.)*

And the elderly
Uncles
And kind
Aunt Jane
Will go
To tea
With the children
Again?

ELIZABETH GODLEY

*Knight Commander of the Bath

Jemima

There was a little girl, who had a little curl
   Right in the middle of her forehead,
And when she was good she was very, very good,
   But when she was bad she was horrid.

She stood on her head, on her little truckle-bed,
   With nobody by for her to hinder;
She screamed and she squalled, she yelled and she bawled,
   And drummed her little heels against the winder.

Her mother heard the noise, and thought it was the boys
   Playing in the empty attic,
She rushed upstairs, and caught her unawares,
   And spanked her, most emphatic.

HENRY WADSWORTH LONGFELLOW, FIRST STANZA
(Other Stanzas Anonymous)

Jim,

WHO RAN AWAY FROM HIS NURSE,
AND WAS EATEN BY A LION

There was a Boy whose name was Jim;
His Friends were very good to him.
They gave him Tea, and Cakes, and Jam,
And slices of delicious Ham,
And Chocolate with pink inside,
And little Tricycles to ride,
And
    read him Stories through and through,
And even took him to the Zoo—
But there it was the dreadful Fate
Befell him, which I now relate.

You know—at least you *ought* to know,
For I have often told you so—
That Children never are allowed
To leave their Nurses in a Crowd;
Now this was Jim's especial Foible,
He ran away when he was able,
And on this inauspicious day
He slipped his hand and ran away!
He hadn't gone a yard when—
                Bang!
With open Jaws, a Lion sprang,
And hungrily began to eat
The Boy: beginning at his feet.

Now just imagine how it feels
When first your toes and then your heels,
And then by gradual degrees,
Your shins and ankles, calves and knees,
Are slowly eaten, bit by bit.

No wonder Jim detested it!
No wonder that he shouted "Hi!"
The Honest Keeper heard his cry,
Though very fat
               he almost ran
To help the little gentleman.
"Ponto!" he ordered as he came
(For Ponto was the Lion's name),
"Ponto!" he cried,
                with angry frown.
"Let go, Sir! Down, Sir! Put it down!"

The Lion made a sudden Stop,
He let the Dainty Morsel drop,
And slunk reluctant to his Cage,
Snarling with Disappointed Rage

But when he bent him over Jim
The Honest Keeper's
                    Eyes were dim.
The Lion having reached his Head,
The Miserable Boy was dead!

When Nurse informed his Parents, they
Were more Concerned than I can say:—
His Mother, as She dried her eyes,
Said, "Well—it gives me no surprise,
He would not do as he was told!"
His Father, who was self-controlled,
Bade all the children round attend
To James' miserable end,
And always keep a-hold of Nurse
For fear of finding something worse.

HILAIRE BELLOC

Sarah Cynthia Sylvia Stout

Sarah Cynthia Sylvia Stout
would not take the garbage out!
She'd boil the water
and open the cans
and scrub the pots
and scour the pans
and grate the cheese
and shell the peas
and mash the yams
and spice the hams,
and make the jams.
But though her daddy
would scream and shout,
she would not take the garbage out.
And so it piled up to the ceilings:
Coffee grounds, potato peelings,
mouldy bread and withered greens,

olive pits and soggy beans,
cracker boxes, chicken bones,
clamshells, eggshells, stale scones,
sour milk and mushy plums,
crumbly cake and cookie crumbs.
At last the garbage piled so high
that finally it reached the sky.
And none of her friends
would come to play.
And all the neighbours moved away.
And finally Sarah Cynthia Stout
said, "I'll take the garbage out!"
But then, of course, it was too late.
The garbage reached beyond the state,
from Memphis to the Golden Gate.
And Sarah met an awful fate,
which I cannot right now relate
because the hour is much too late.
But, children, think of Sarah Stout
and always take the garbage out!

SHELLEY SILVERSTEIN

What the Lord High Chamberlain Said

Little Prince Carl he stole away
    From the gold-laced guard and the powdered page,
And the ladies in waiting, who night and day
    Kept their bird in a gilded cage.

Alone in the twilight grey and dim,
    He climbed on the carven chair of state,
And there with a smile sufficiently grim,
    And a royal air, His Highness sate.

He folded his arms with a mighty mien,—
    Little Prince Carl, the son of a king,—
But never an auditor was to be seen,
    Save the pea-green cockatoo, perched in his swing!

And rebellion shone in His Highness' eyes:
    "When I am a king full-grown," said he,
"I fear there is going to be surprise
    At some of the things this court shall see!

"With the Dowager Duchess I shall begin;
    When I say, 'Stand forth!' she shall bow her low.
'For me to jump you have said was a sin;
    I command *you* to jump wherever you go!'

"The Court Physician I next shall take:
    'And you, I hear, have declared it best
That I, your monarch, shall not eat cake,—
    Plum-cake, too, of the very best!—

" 'Well, *you* are to eat a gallon of rice,
    And nothing besides, for every meal;
I am sure 'tis quite "wholesome," "nourishing," "nice,"
    But I know quite well just how you feel!'

"Now let the Lord Chamberlain have a care!"
    His Highness' voice took a terrible ring;

He rumpled his curls of yellow hair,
  And the pea-green cockatoo shook in its swing!

" 'Down! Get down on your knocking knees,
  Down with your smile and your snuff-box, too!'
I will thunder, and now 'tis time, if you please,
  To settle an old, old score with you!

" 'What became of those three white mice
  That crept from the royal nursery door,
After you said if they did it twice
  They should never be heard of anymore?

" '*I know, for I heard the little one squeak!*
  And I ran and stopped my ears up tight.
You need not squirm, and you need not speak,
  For your fate shall be settled this very night.

" 'In the darkest depths of the dungeon lone
  You are to live, but do not fear,
For company livelier than your own
  You shall have three million mice a year!' "

The little prince clapped his hands in glee,
  And laughed aloud at this fancying,—
Oh, a rare and a wonderful monarch he!—
  And the pea-green cockatoo hopped in its swing:

When out of the twilight a slow voice rolled;
   There stood the High Chamberlain, stern, who said:
"I regret to state that I've just been told
   It is time for Your Highness to go to bed!"

And lo! not a word did His Highness say!—
   He went at once, like the son of a king.
But his bright curls drooped as he walked away,
   And the cockatoo's head went under its wing.

VIRGINIA WOODWARD CLOUD

Maria Jane

It really gives me heartfelt pain
To tell you of Maria Jane,
For oh! she was so naughty!
Her nurse would weep and say: "Ah me!
If you're so bad when only three,
What will you be at forty?"

She loved to paddle in the wet
'Till soaked with mud her clothes would get,
For oh! she was so dirty!

Her nurse would weep and cry: "Ah me!
If you love dirt so much at three,
What will you love at thirty?"

Her appetite did all surprise,
Plum puddings, cakes and hot mince-pies,
For oh! she ne'er had plenty!
Her nurse would weep and scream: "Ah me!
If you can eat so much at three,
What will you eat at twenty?"

ALFRED SCOTT-GATTY

The Story of Johnny Head-in-Air

As he trudged along to school,
It was always Johnny's rule
To be looking at the sky
And the clouds that floated by;
But what just before him lay,
In his way,
Johnny never thought about;
So that every one cried out—
"Look at little Johnny there,
Little Johnny Head-in-Air!"

Running just in Johnny's way,
Came a little dog one day;
Johnny's eyes were still astray
Up on high,
In the sky;
And he never heard them cry—
"Johnny, mind, the dog is nigh!"
Bump!
Dump!

Down they fell, with such a thump,
Dog and Johnny in a lump!

Once, with head as high as ever,
Johnny walked beside the river.
Johnny watched the swallows trying
Which was cleverest at flying.
Oh! what fun!
Johnny watched the bright round sun
Going in and coming out;
This was all he thought about.
So he strode on, only think!
To the river's very brink,
Where the bank was high and steep.
And the water very deep;
And the fishes, in a row,
Stared to see him coming so.

One step more! Oh! sad to tell!
Headlong in Poor Johnny fell.

And the fishes, in dismay,
Wagged their tails and ran away.

There lay Johnny on his face,
With his nice red writing-case;
But as they were passing by,
Two strong men had heard him cry;
And, with sticks, these two strong men
Hooked poor Johnny out again.
Oh! you should have seen him shiver
When they pull'd him from the river.
He was in a sorry plight!
Dripping wet, and such a fright!
Wet all over, everywhere,
Clothes, and arms, and face, and hair;
Johnny never will forget
What it is to be so wet.

And the fishes, one, two, three,
Are come back again, you see,
Up they came the moment after,
To enjoy the fun and laughter.
Each popped out his little head,
And, to tease poor Johnny, said,
"Silly little Johnny, look,
You have lost your writing-book!"

HEINRICH HOFFMANN

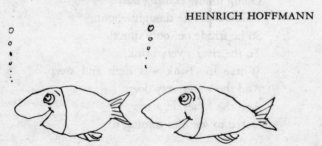

from An Alphabet of Famous Goops

Bohunkus would Take Off his Hat, and Bow and Smile, and
Things like That.
His Face and Hair were Always Neat, and when he Played he
did not Cheat;
But Oh! what Awful Words he Said, when it was Time to Go
to Bed!

Ezekiel, so his Parents said, just Simply Loved to Go to Bed;
He was as Quiet as could Be whenever there were Folks to Tea;
And yet, he had a Little Way of Grumbling, when he should
Obey.

When Festus was but Four Years Old his Parents Seldom had to
Scold;
They never Called him "Festus Don't!" he Never Whined and
said "I Won't!"
Yet it was Sad to See him Dine. His Table Manners were Not
Fine.

How Interesting Isaac Seemed! He never Fibbed, he Seldom
Screamed;
His Company was Quite a Treat to all the Children on the Street;
But Nurse has Told me of his Wrath when he was Made to Take
a Bath!

Some think that Obadiah's Charm was that he Never Tried to
Harm
Dumb Animals in any Way, though Some are Cruel when they
Play.
But though he was so Sweet and Kind, his Mother found him
Slow to Mind.

Uriah Never Licked his Knife, nor Sucked his Fingers, in his
　Life.
He Never Reached, to Help Himself, the Sugar Bowl upon the
　Shelf.
He Never Popped his Cherry Pits; but he had Horrid Sulky Fits!

The Zealous Zibeon was Such as Casual Callers Flatter Much.
His Maiden Aunts would Say, with Glee, "How Good, how Pure,
　how Dear is He!"
And Yet, he Drove his Mother Crazy—he was so Slow, he was so
　Lazy!

GELETT BURGESS

The Contrary Boy

I am the queerest sort of boy the world has ever seen—
In fact, I don't suppose before my like has ever been,
Because, from early dawning to the setting of the sun,
I always want to do the things that really can't be done.

For instance, when the summer comes, I sit down by the gate
And almost tear my hair with rage because I cannot skate.
And through the heated August nights I often lie in bed
And moan and groan because I can't go coasting on my sled.

Then when the frigid winter's here, and things begin to freeze,
I feel as though I'd like to climb up in the apple trees
And pluck the blossoms from the twigs; but blossoms none are
　there
When winter winds are blowing and the apple boughs are bare.

At breakfast time I sit me down, and often deeply sigh
Because there's toast and buckwheat cakes instead of pumpkin pie;
Yet, when at dinner time we've pie, my tears come down like
  lakes
Because by that time I've a taste for toast and buckwheat cakes.

And I would say to other boys who think it's fun to be
Contrariwise that they would best take warning now from me,
Because I find the habit leaves me always dull and sad,
And makes of me a very drear, ill-natured sort of lad.

GASTON V. DRAKE

Taffy

Taffy was a Welshman, Taffy was a thief,
Taffy came to my house and stole a piece of beef;
I went to Taffy's house, Taffy wasn't in,
I jumped upon his Sunday hat, and poked it with a pin.

Taffy was a Welshman, Taffy was a sham,
Taffy came to my house and stole a leg of lamb;
I went to Taffy's house, Taffy was away,
I stuffed his socks with sawdust and filled his shoes with clay.

Taffy was a Welshman, Taffy was a cheat,
Taffy came to my house and stole a piece of meat;
I went to Taffy's house, Taffy was not there,
I hung his coat and trousers to roast before a fire.

ANONYMOUS

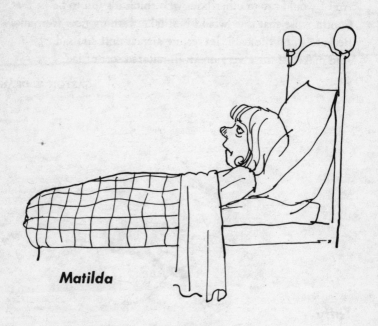

Matilda

Matilda got her stockings wet,
And the result was, I regret,
Because she wouldn't change when told,
Matilda caught a dreadful cold.
Matilda sniffed and snuffled and sneezed,
Matilda choked and croaked and wheezed,
And the doctor came, and the doctor said
Matilda was to go to bed.
He sent her lozenges and lotions,
Some to be taken straight away,
And others three times every day,

With iodine to paint her skin,
And embrocation to rub in:
In fact, you might almost have filled a
Cart with the things he sent Matilda.
And yet Matilda, if you please,
Disliked the doctor's remedies.
Oh dear! there was a dreadful scene
Each time Matilda took quinine:
Matilda's yells came fast and faster
When they put on a mustard plaster:
Matilda's screams were even louder
When she was given Gregory's powder,
And it took half an hour's toil
To make her swallow castor oil.
I have known other painful cases,
But never seen such awful faces
As those that young Matilda made
On every visit the doctor paid.
What can you do with so self-willed a
Person as the girl Matilda?

*   *   *

The other day I had a letter
To say Matilda was no better;
And from the way that she's behaving
Matilda doesn't seem worth saving.
Unless Matilda mends her ways
Upon the tombstone that they raise
Will be the words: "Here lies Matilda.
Nothing but naughty temper killed her."

F. GWYNNE EVANS

HERE ⇩
LIES
MATILDA
nothing but
naughty temper
killed her.
ha ha!

Never Stew Your Sister

Brother and Sister

"Sister, sister, go to bed!
Go and rest your weary head."
Thus the prudent brother said.

"Do you want a battered hide,
Or scratches to your face applied?"
Thus his sister calm replied.

"Sister, do not raise my wrath.
I'd make you into mutton broth
As easily as kill a moth!"

The sister raised her beaming eye
And looked on him indignantly
And sternly answered, "Only try!"

Off to the cook he quickly ran.
"Dear Cook, please lend a frying-pan
To me as quickly as you can."

"And wherefore should I lend it you?"
"The reason, Cook, is plain to view.
I wish to make an Irish stew."

"What meat is in that stew to go?"
"My sister'll be the contents!"

"Oh!"
"You'll lend the pan to me, Cook?"

"No!"

Moral: Never stew your sister.

LEWIS CARROLL

from A Children's Don't

Don't tell Papa his nose is red
   As any rosebud or geranium,
Forbear to eye his hairless head
   Or criticise his cootlike cranium;
'Tis years of sorrow and of care
   Have made his head come through his hair.

Don't ask your uncle why he's fat;
   Avoid upon his toe-joints treading;
Don't hide a hedgehog in his hat,
   He will not see the slightest sport
In pepper put into his port!

Don't pull away the cherished chair
    On which Mamma intended sitting,
Not yet prepare her session there
    By setting on the seat her knitting;
Pause ere you hurt her spine, I pray—
    That is a game that *two* can play.

HARRY GRAHAM

Wilhelmina Mergenthaler

Wilhelmina Mergenthaler
Had a lovely ermine collar
Made of just the nicest fur,
That her mamma bought for her.
Once, when mamma was away,
Out a-shopping for the day,
        Wilhelmina Mergenthaler
        Ate her lovely ermine collar.

HARRY P. TABER

Science for the Young

Thoughtful little Willie Frazer
Carved his name with father's razor;
Father, unaware of trouble,
Used the blade to shave his stubble.
Father cut himself severely,
Which pleased little Willie dearly—
"I have fixed my father's razor
So it cuts!" said Willie Frazer

Mamie often wondered why
Acids trouble alkali—
Mamie, in a manner placid,
Fed the cat boracic acid,
Whereupon the cat grew frantic,
Executing many an antic,
"Ah!" cried Mamie, overjoyed,
"Pussy is an alkaloid!"

Arthur with a lighted taper
Touched the fire to grandpa's paper.
Grandpa leaped a foot or higher,
Dropped the sheet and shouted "Fire!"
Arthur, wrapped in contemplation,
Viewed the scene of conflagration.
"This," he said, "confirms my notion—
Heat creates both light and motion."

Wee, experimental Nina
Dropped her mother's Dresden china
From a seventh-story casement,
Smashing, crashing to the basement.
Nina, somewhat apprehensive,
Said: "This china is expensive,
Yet it proves by demonstration
Newton's law of gravitation."

WALLACE IRWIN

93

Sister Nell

In the family drinking well
Willie pushed his sister Nell.
She's there yet, because it kilt her—
Now we have to buy a filter.

ANONYMOUS

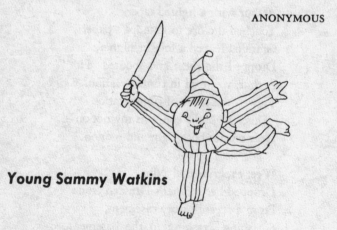

Young Sammy Watkins

Young Sammy Watkins jumped out of bed;
He ran to his sister and cut off her head.
This gave his dear mother a great deal of pain;
She hopes that he never will do it again.

ANONYMOUS

Careless Willie

Willie, with a thirst for gore,
Nailed his sister to the door.
Mother said, with humor quaint:
"Now, Willie dear, don't scratch the paint."

ANONYMOUS

Three Bad Ones

Tom tied a kettle to the tail of a cat,
Jill put a stone in the blind man's hat,
Bob threw his grandmother down the stairs—
And they all grew up ugly, and nobody cares.

ENGLISH NURSERY RHYME

Our Polite Parents

SEDATE MAMMA

When guests were present, dear little Mabel
  Climbed right up on the dinner-table
And naughtily stood upon her head!
  "I wouldn't do that, dear," Mamma said.

MERRY MOSES

Merry, funny little Moses
  Burnt off both his brothers' noses;
And it made them look so queer
  Mamma said, "Why, Moses, dear!"

JOHNNY'S FUN

Johnny climbed up on the bed,
    And hammered nails in Mamma's head.
Though the child was much elated,
    Mamma felt quite irritated.

A MERRY GAME

Betty and Belinda Ames
    Had the pleasantest of games;
'Twas to hide from one another
    Marmaduke, their baby brother.
Once Belinda, little love,
    Hid the baby in the stove;
Such a joke! for little Bet
    Hasn't found the baby yet.

TOM AND GRANDPA

From his toes up to his shins
    Tom stuck Grandpa full of pins;
Although Tom the fun enjoyed,
    Grandpapa was quite annoyed.

BABY'S LOOKS

Bobby with the nursery shears
   Cut off both the baby's ears;
At the baby, so unsightly,
   Mamma raised her eyebrows slightly.

JEANETTE'S PRANKS

One night, Jeanette, a roguish little lass,
   Sneaked in the guest room and turned on the gas;
When morning dawned the guest was dead in bed,
   But "Children will be children," Mamma said.

CAROLYN WELLS

Good and Bad Children

Children, you are very little,
And your bones are very brittle;
If you would grow great and stately,
You must try to walk sedately.

You must still be bright and quiet,
And content with simple diet;

And remain, through all bewild'ring,
Innocent and honest children.

Happy hearts and happy faces,
Happy play in grassy places—
That was how, in ancient ages,
Children grew to kings and sages.

But the unkind and the unruly,
And the sort who eat unduly,
They must never hope for glory—
Theirs is quite a different story!

Cruel children, crying babies,
All grow up as geese and gabies,
Hated, as their age increases,
By their nephews and their nieces.

ROBERT LOUIS STEVENSON

The Stern Parent

Father heard his Children scream,
So he threw them in the stream,
Saying, as he drowned the third,
"Children should be seen, *not* heard!"

HARRY GRAHAM

Willie

Willie had a purple monkey climbing up a yellow stick
And when he sucked the paint all off it made him deathly sick;
And in his latest hours he clasped that monkey in his hand,
And bade good-bye to earth and went into a better land.

Oh! no more he'll shoot his sister with his little wooden gun;
And no more he'll twist the pussy's tail and make her yowl, for
   fun.
The pussy's tail now stands out straight; the gun is laid aside;
The monkey doesn't jump around since little Willie died.

MAX ADELER

Run, Kitty, Run!

Do you suppose it's really really true
That cats have got more lives than me and you?
So many, many times I've heard it said
A cat is hardly ever really dead.

And even when it seems to be it's not.
You never know *how* many lives it's got
There may be four or five or even nine—

* * *

I think I'll go and try it out on mine!

JIMMY GARTHWAITE

And Beat Him
When He Sneezes

The Duchess' Lullaby

Speak roughly to your little boy,
    And beat him when he sneezes:
He only does it to annoy,
    Because he knows it teases.

LEWIS CARROLL

Dirge for a Bad Boy

Richard has been sent to bed:
Let a solemn dirge be said.
Sent to bed before his time,
Sentenced for a nursery crime.
Draw down the blinds in every room
And fill the dismal house with gloom.
Richard has been sent to bed:
Let a solemn dirge be said.

Tell the cat and kitten they
Must cease from their unseemly play.
Stop the telephone from ringing;
Stop the kettle from its singing.
And hark, is that the Hoover's hum?
Let the Hoover too be dumb.

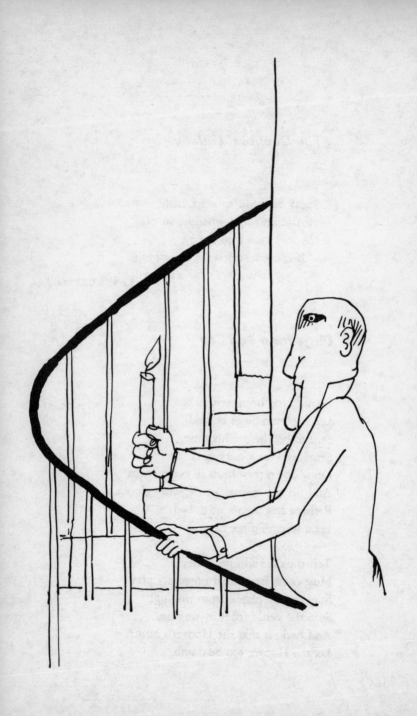

Richard has been sent to bed:
Let a solemn dirge be said.

Turn off, turn off, the central heat,
And let the cold creep round our feet.
Put out the fire and let it die
Underneath that juicy pie,
That we may eat (if eat we must)
Cold apple and a colder crust.
Richard has been sent to bed:
Let a solemn dirge be said.

And when the time has come for all
To follow through the darkened hall,
Let every sound of mirth be banned—
Take each a candle in his hand,
And winding up the stairway slow
In melancholy order go,
While this solemn dirge is said
For a poor sinner in his bed.

E. V. RIEU

Self-Sacrifice

Father, chancing to chastise
   His indignant daughter Sue,
Said, "I hope you realise
   That this hurts me more than you."

Susan straightway ceased to roar;
   "If that's really true," said she,
"I can stand a good deal more;
   Pray go on, and don't mind me."

HARRY GRAHAM

The Cruel Naughty Boy

There was a cruel naughty boy,
   Who sat upon the shore,
A-catching little fishes by
   The dozen and the score.

And as they squirmed and wriggled there,
   He shouted loud with glee,
"You surely cannot want to live,
   You're little-er than me."

Just then with a malicious leer,
   And a capacious smile,
Before him from the water deep
   There rose a crocodile.

He eyed the little naughty boy,
    Then heaved a blubbering sigh,
And said, "You cannot want to live,
    You're little-er than I."

The fishes squirm and wriggle still,
    Beside that sandy shore,
The cruel little naughty boy,
    Was never heard of more.

ANONYMOUS

Thief

A maiden caught stealing a dahlia,
Said, "Oh, you shan't tell on me, shahlia?"
    But the florist was hot,
    And he said, "Like as not
They'll send you to jail, you bad gahlia."

ANONYMOUS

Piano Practice

A doting father once there was
  Who loved his daughter Gerda,
Until she got the piano craze—
  Then how the passion stirred her!
Her fingers were wild elephants' feet,
  And as month after month he heard her
    He tried every way
    To stop her play
From bribery to murder.

One day when she was practising,
  He popped up behind and caught her
And dumped her in his wheelbarrow
  And carried her off to slaughter.

Tipping her into a well, he cried,
"Hurrah! I've drowned my daughter!"
But a voice from the well
Rang out like a bell,
"Aha—there isn't any water!"

IAN SERRAILLIER

Godfrey Gordon Gustavus Gore

Godfrey Gordon Gustavus Gore—
No doubt you have heard the name before—
Was a boy who never would shut a door!

The wind might whistle, the wind might roar,
And teeth be aching and throats be sore,
But still he never would shut the door.

His father would beg, his mother implore,
"Godfrey Gordon Gustavus Gore,
We really *do* wish you would shut the door!"

Their hands they wrung, their hair they tore;
But Godfrey Gordon Gustavus Gore
Was deaf as the buoy out at the Nore.

When he walked forth the folks would roar,
"Godfrey Gordon Gustavus Gore,
Why don't you think to shut the door?"

They rigged out a Shutter with sail and oar,
And threatened to pack off Gustavus Gore
On a voyage of penance to Singapore.

But he begged for mercy, and said, "No more!
Pray do not send me to Singapore
On a Shutter, and then I will shut the door!"

"You will?" said his parents; "then keep on shore!
But mind you do! For the plague is sore
Of a fellow that never will shut the door,
Godfrey Gordon Gustavus Gore!"

WILLIAM BRIGHTY RANDS

Little Orphant Annie

Little Orphant Annie's come to our house to stay,
An' wash the cups and saucers up, an' brush the crumbs away,
An' shoo the chickens off the porch, an' dust the hearth, an' sweep,
An' make the fire, an' bake the bread, an' earn her board-an'-keep;
An' all us other children, when the supper things is done,
We set around the kitchen fire an' has the mostest fun
A-list'nin' to the witch-tales 'at Annie tells about,
An' the Gobble-uns 'at gits you
        Ef you
            Don't
                Watch
                    Out!

Onc't there was a little boy wouldn't say his pray'rs—
An' when he went to bed at night, away up stairs,
His mammy heerd him holler, an' his daddy heerd him bawl,
An' when they turn't the kivvers down, he wasn't there at all!
An' they seeked him in the rafter-room, an' cubby-hole, an' press,
An' seeked him up the chimbly-flue, an' ever'wheres, I guess;
But all they ever found was thist his pants an' roundabout!
An' the Gobble-uns'll git you
        Ef you
            Don't
                Watch
                    Out!

An' one time a little girl 'ud allus laugh an' grin,
An' make fun of Ever' one, an' all her blood-an'-kin;
An' onc't when they was "company," an' ole folks was there,
She mocked 'em an' shocked 'em, an' said she didn't care!
An' thist as she kicked her heels, an' turn't to run an' hide,
They was two great big Black Things a-standin' by her side,

An' they snatched her through the ceilin' 'fore she knowed what
  she's about!
An' the Gobble-uns'll git you
      Ef you
         Don't
            Watch
               Out!

An' little Orphant Annie says, when the blaze is blue,
An' the lampwick sputters, an' the wind goes woo-oo!
An' you hear the crickets quit, an' the moon is grey,
An' the lightnin'-bugs in dew is all squenched away,—
You better mind yer parents, and yer teachers fond and dear,
An' churish them 'at loves you, an' dry the orphant's tear,
An' he'p the pore an' needy ones 'at clusters all about,
Er the Gobble-uns'll git you
      Ef you
         Don't
            Watch
               Out!

JAMES WHITCOMB RILEY

Belsnickel

Santa Claus comes when you're good
    With candy and toys in his sleigh,
But if you don't do as you should,
    Belsnickel will take them away.
His nose is curved round like a sickle,
                 Belsnickel.

He flies from the Antarctic Pole
    As soon as he hears you've been bad,

To carry away to his hole
　　The very best gifts that you had.
His mouth is as sour as a pickle,
　　　　　　　　　Belsnickel.

He comes on his leathery wings,
　　But though you've been naughty, he sighs;
He never likes taking your things;
　　The tears trickle down from his eyes,
And trickle, and trickle, and trickle,
　　　　　　　　　Belsnickel.

But if you don't quarrel or fight
    Or grumble or whimper or groan,
Belsnickel is happy and bright
    And leaves all your presents alone.
So act in the way that will tickle
                    Belsnickel.

ARTHUR GUITERMAN

Adolphus Elfinstone

Adolphus Elfinstone of Nachez,
Thought it fun to play with matches
Until the little Goop had learned
It hurt a lot when he got burned!
A *little* fire is queer and curious;
But soon it grows quite big and furious.

GELETT BURGESS

Author and Title Index

Author index

Anonymous (cont.)

Title index

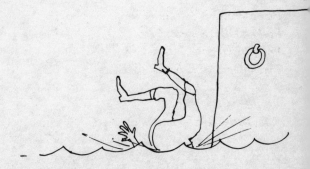

Adrian Henri

Phantom Lollipop Lady

A sparkling collection of poems especially
for children by one of Britain's best-known
poets.

'A new collection of poems is like a box of
assorted chocolates . . . Adrian Henri's new
collection is a very tasty selection. Open this
tempting book yourselves and pick out your
best ones . . .'

Adele Geras

'A terrific read'

Parents

A Selected List of Humour and Poetry from Mammoth

While every effort is made to keep prices low, it is sometimes necessary to increase prices at short notice. Mammoth Books reserves the right to show new retail prices on covers which may differ from those previously advertised in the text or elsewhere.

The prices shown below were correct at the time of going to press.